DEPARTMENT OF THE NAVY
HEADQUARTERS UNITED STATES MARINE CORPS
3000 MARINE CORPS PENTAGON
WASHINGTON, DC 20350-3000

INCENTIVE AWARDS PROGRAM FOR HQMC CIVILIANS

MCO 12451.3B
ARH
AUG 2 6 2009

Marine Corps Order 12451.3B

From: Commandant of the Marine Corps
To: Distribution List

Subj: INCENTIVE AWARDS PROGRAM FOR HQMC CIVILIANS

Ref: (a) DOD 1400.25-M, Subchapter 451, "DOD Civilian Personnel
          Manual," December 1, 1996
      (b) DON Human Resources Implementation Guidance,
          Subchapter 451.1
      (c) MCO 12451.2C
      (d) SECNAV M-5210.1

Encl: (1) Guide to Civilian Awards and Recognition

1. <u>Situation</u>. To provide policy and procedural guidance for
recognizing HQMC civilian employees through the incentive awards
program, per references (a) through (d).

2. <u>Cancellation</u>. MCO 12451.3A.

3. <u>Mission</u>. Enclosure (1) provides policy, procedural
guidance, and delegations of authority to approve incentive
awards for HQMC civilians.

4. <u>Execution</u>

    a. <u>Commander's Intent and Concept of Operations</u>

        (1) <u>Commander's Intent</u>. This guide is intended to
provide HQMC supervisors and managers with a consolidated source
of information on the various awards that are available to HQMC
civilians. This guide does not cover every award available, but
it does cover the primary monetary and non-monetary awards
civilians may receive. Information about other awards available
to civilians can be obtained from the Employee Management
Advisory Services Section, Human Resources and Organizational
Management Branch (HROM).

(2) Concept of Operations. Incentive awards will be used to recognize the accomplishments and superior achievements of civilians to promote excellence in performance. Refer to appendix A of enclosure (1) for a matrix of approval authorities for the various awards addressed.

b. Subordinate Element Missions

(1) HQMC Managers and Supervisors. Shall provide appropriate recognition to civilian employees for their achievements and accomplishments, and for other reasons as cited in enclosure (1).

(2) Electronic Forms. All forms contained in enclosure (1) are available on the Marine Corps Electronic Forms System (MCEFS) website at http://192.156.19.109/ar/MCEFS.nsf.

5. Administration and Logistics. Recommendations concerning the content of this order may be forwarded to the CMC (ARH) via the appropriate chain of command.

6. Command and Signal

a. Command. This Order is applicable to HQMC civilians.

b. Signal. This Order is effective the date signed.

A. A. WASHINGTON
By direction

DISTRIBUTION: PCN 10212082800

Copy to: 7000260 (2)
7000144/8145001 (1)

2

LOCATOR SHEET

Subj: INCENTIVE AWARDS PROGRAM FOR HQMC CIVILIANS

Location: _____
          Indicate the location(s) of the copy(ies) of this
Order.

RECORD OF CHANGES

Log completed change action as indicated.

Change Number	Date of Change	Date Entered	Signature of Person Incorporating Change

TABLE OF CONTENTS

TABLE OF CONTENTS

TABLE OF CONTENTS

TABLE OF CONTENTS

Chapter 1

Special Act and On The Spot Awards

1. <u>General</u>. Special Act awards are cash awards designed to recognize group or individual achievements of a non-recurring nature. These achievements may be within or outside the employee's normal job responsibilities, and recognize efforts and results that go significantly beyond what is expected. Special Act awards are used to recognize exceptional accomplishments, such as outstanding achievement, and may be given at any time. To the extent practicable, Special Act awards should be made as close as possible to the special act upon which the award is based. An On the Spot award is the same as a Special Act award but is limited to $750, and is generally used to recognize one time achievements that have resulted in service or a work product of an exceptionally high quality or quantity.

2. <u>Eligibility</u>. All civilians are eligible for Special Act and On The Spot awards.

3. <u>Criteria for Granting Special Act and On The Spot Awards</u>

    a. Achievements upon which Special Act and On The Spot awards are based must produce tangible or intangible benefits to the organization that improve the efficiency, economy, or effectiveness of government operations. Special Act awards may also be based on scientific achievements or on an act of heroism.

    b. A written justification is required to support all nominations for Special Act and On The Spot awards. The justification must fully and clearly identify the contributions of the employee and identify the tangible or intangible benefits associated with the contributions.

4. <u>Determining Award Amounts</u>. Except as noted below, Special Act award amounts will be determined in accordance with Table 1-1 for awards based on tangible benefits, Table 1-2 for awards based on intangible benefits; or a combination thereof. The range for On The Spot award amounts is $25 to $750; the amount of the award will be commensurate with the nature of the act or service being recognized. Summer hires are eligible for special act awards of up to $300 per individual.

5. Nomination Form. Use the form at appendix B to submit nominations for Special Act and On The Spot cash awards.

6. Approval of Special Act and On The Spot Awards

    a. A matrix of approval authorities for the award and amount is provided in appendix A of this guide.

    b. The approval authority may not be re-delegated to a lower organizational level for awards of $751 to $2,000 per individual.

7. Submission of Awards. All Special Act Awards will be submitted to AR Fiscal to certify that funds are available prior to submission to HROM for processing. All required approvals must be obtained prior to submission.

8. Records Management

    a. Records documenting On The Spot and Special Act Awards maintained at the Deputy Commandant/Director Marine Corps Staff level and below shall be maintained per reference (d) SSIC 12450.1a and 1b as appropriate.

    b. Records documenting On The Spot and Special Act Awards maintained at the Commandant of the Marine Corps level and above shall be maintained per reference (d) SSIC 12450.5.

ESTIMATED FIRST-YEAR BENEFITS TO THE GOVERNMENT	AMOUNT OF AWARD*
Up to $10,000 in benefits	10% of benefits
Between $10,000 and $100,000 in benefits	$1,000 plus 3% to 10% of benefits over $10,000
More than $100,000 in benefits	$3,700 to $10,000 for the first $100,000 in benefits plus 0.5% to 1% of benefits above $100,00

Table 1-1.--Scale of Award Amounts for Special Act Awards Based on Tangible Benefits

*Note: Presidential approval is required for all individual Special Act Awards of more than $25,000. Recommendations must

be reviewed and approved by the Department of Navy Awards Review Panel, the SECNAV, the SECDEF, and the Office of Personnel Management.

VALUE OF BENEFIT ↓	EXTENT OF APPLICATION			
	LIMITED Affects functions, mission or personnel of one facility, installation, regional area or an organizational element of headquarters; affects a small area of science or technology	**EXTENDED** Affects functions, mission, or personnel of an entire regional area, command or bureau; affects an important area of science or technology	**BROAD** Affects functions, mission, or personnel of several regional areas or commands, or an entire department or agency; affects an extensive area of science or technology	**GENERAL** Affects functions, mission, or personnel of more than one department or agency or is in the public interest throughout the nation and beyond
MODERATE Change or modification of an operating principle or procedure with limited impact or use	$25-$500	$501-$750	$751-$1,000	$1,001-$1,500
SUBSTANTIAL Substantial change or modification of procedures; an important improvement to the value of a product, activity, program or service to the public	$501-$750	$751-$1,000	$1,001-$1,500	$1,501 - $3,150
HIGH Complete revision of a basic principle or procedure; a highly significant improvement to the value of a product or service	$751-$1,000	$1,001-$1,500	$1,501-$3,150	$3,151 - $6,300
EXCEPTIONAL Initiation of a new principle or major procedure; a superior improvement to the quality of a critical product, activity, program, or service to the public	$1,001-$1,500	$1,501-$3,150	$3,151-$6,300	$6,301-$10,000

Table 1-2.--Scale of Award Amounts for Special Act Awards Based on Intangible Benefits

Chapter 2

Time Off Awards

1. <u>General</u>. A Time Off Award is designed to recognize superior accomplishments of employees with time off from duty, without a loss of pay or charge to leave. A Time Off Award may be based on sustained high level performance or may be based on accomplishments that are similar in nature to those recognized with Special Act awards.

2. <u>Eligibility</u>. All civilian employees are eligible for a Time Off Award.

3. <u>Criteria for Granting Time Off Awards</u>. Time Off Awards may be used alone or in combination with other awards to recognize employee contributions as follows:

    a. Making a high quality contribution involving a difficult or important project or assignment;

    b. Displaying special initiative and skill in completing an assignment or project before the deadline;

    c. Ensuring, or helping to ensure, that the mission of the unit is accomplished during a difficult period by completing additional work over and above usual duties.

    d. Using initiative or creativity by making improvements in a product, activity, program, or service;

    e. Sustaining a high level of performance for an extended period of time.

4. <u>Approval of Time Off Awards</u>

    a. A Time Off Award of 8 hours or less may be approved by the immediate supervisor, without further review and approval. Time Off Awards of 9 to 24 hours may be approved by the Branch Heads; Time Off Awards of 25-80 hours may be approved by Division Heads and above.

    b. All Time Off Awards, including those based on sustained high level performance, must be supported by a written justification which fully describes the achievements upon which the Time Off Award is based and which explains how the number of time off award hours were determined.

5. <u>Limitations on Time Off Awards</u>. A maximum of 80 Time Off Award hours may be granted in a leave year; no more than 40 hours may be approved based on a single contribution. Time Off Awards must be used within one calendar year from the date of approval. Any hours not taken within one calendar year will be forfeited and will not, under any circumstance, be converted to cash or restored to the employee. Further, time off may not be transferred between DOD components, to another federal agency, or to another employee under the Voluntary Leave Transfer Program. Time Off Award hours may be transferred within the Department of the Navy. Time Off Awards may not be awarded to create the effect of a holiday or treated as administrative excusals or leave (e.g., they may not be awarded in conjunction with a military "down" or training day or the like).

6. <u>Determining Time Off Awards Amounts</u>

　　a. The Time Off Awards Table (see table 2-1) is the suggested method to determine time off award amounts.

　　b. When determining whether to grant a Time Off Award, also consider whether the employee currently has "use or lose" annual leave available. Since a Time Off Award may not be converted to cash under any circumstance, it may not be in the best interest of the employee or the organization to approve Time Off Awards for employees who have significant amounts of use or lose leave.

7. <u>Other Information</u>. Time Off Awards may be granted in addition to and in conjunction with, other awards, including NSPS performance based cash bonuses and salary increases.

8. <u>Nomination Form</u>. Use the form at appendix C to submit nominations for Time Off Awards.

9. <u>Records Management</u>. Records documenting Time Off Awards submitted to the Deputy Commandant/Director Marine Corps Staff level and below shall be maintained per reference (d) SSIC 12450.1a.

TIME OFF AWARDS TABLE*	
VALUE TO THE ORGANIZATION	**NUMBER OF TIME OFF AWARD HOURS**
MODERATE: A contribution to a product, activity, program or service which is of sufficient value to warrant formal recognition or a beneficial change or modification of operating principles or procedures	1 to 10
SUBSTANTIAL: An important contribution to the value of a product, activity program or service to the public or a significant change in operating principles or procedures	11 to 20
HIGH: A highly significant contribution to the value of a product, activity, program or service to the public or a complete revision of operating principles or procedures with considerable impact	21 to 30
EXCEPTIONAL: A superior contribution to the quality of a critical product, activity, program, or service to the public or initiation of a new principle or major procedure with significant impact	31 to 40
EXCEPTIONAL WITH SIGNIFICANT IMPACT ON MISSION AND GOALS: A superior contribution to the quality of a critical product, activity, program, or service to the public or initiation of a new principle or major procedure. Contribution has a significant impact on the mission and goals of the organization and furthers the strategic goals of the Commandant.	41-80

Table 2-1.--Time Off Award Table

*THIS SCALE APPLIES TO FULL TIME EMPLOYEES WITH STANDARD 80-HOUR TOURS OF DUTY. FOR ASSISTANCE IN DETERMINING TIME OFF AWARD AMOUNTS FOR OTHER EMPLOYEES, PLEASE CONTACT HROM.

Chapter 3

Distinguished Civilian Service Award

1. <u>General</u>. The Distinguished Civilian Service Award (DCSA) is the highest honorary award the Secretary of the Navy may confer on a civilian. The DCSA is only granted to those civilians who have given distinguished and/or extraordinary service to the Department of Navy. All recommendations for the DCSA will be submitted on an individual basis. When two or more employees with the same achievement are being nominated for this award, separate nomination packages will be submitted.

2. <u>Nature of the Award</u>. The DCSA consists of a certificate signed by the SECNAV and a medal set.

3. <u>Eligibility</u>. All civilians are eligible for the DCSA.

4. <u>Criteria</u>

a. The service and achievements upon which this award is based must be truly exceptional when measured against the position requirements of the employee and should far exceed the contributions and service of others with comparable responsibilities. The DCSA should be reserved for those civilians whose contributions are so exceptional and/or significant that recognition by the Secretary of the Navy is merited.

b. When the DCSA is based on long time service, one or more of the following indicators will be present:

(1) A pattern of long term sustained high performance as evidenced by the nominee having previously received high honorary awards and a record of consistent performance based awards and recognition.

(2) Career achievements that are recognized throughout the Department of Navy.

(3) Innovative leadership of highly successful programs that have had an impact beyond the nominee's activity or command.

c. When the DCSA is based on one or more accomplishments or achievements, one or more of the following indicators will be present:

(1) Accomplishments or achievements that have had, at a minimum, Navy-wide impact.

(2) Scientific or technical advances or suggestions of significant value.

(3) Major cost savings, reduction, and/or avoidance.

(4) Unusual acts of heroism, successful cooperative efforts with other Department of Navy offices, federal agencies, or the private sector.

5. Approval Process. All nominations for the DCSA will be submitted to M&RA (MPC-10) for review and forwarding to the Marine Corps Incentive Awards Board (MCIAB) for review, approval and forwarding to the CMC for endorsement. If approved by the CMC, the nomination will be forwarded to the SECNAV. The MCIAB was established by the CMC to review high level award nominations submitted by all Marine Corps commands and activities prior to forwarding to the SECNAV for approval.

6. Award Submission Requirements. Appendix D provides information as to what DCSA nominations must include and the format for the nominations.

7. Records Management. Records documenting Distinguished Civilian Service Awards submitted to the Commandant of the Marine Corps and above shall be maintained per reference (d) SSIC 12450.5.

Chapter 4

Superior Civilian Service Award

1. <u>General</u>. The Superior Civilian Service Award (SCSA) is the highest level award which the Commandant of the Marine Corps may bestow on a civilian employee. This award recognizes employee contributions that are exceptionally high in value, but which affect a smaller area than the DCSA.

2. <u>Nature of the Award</u>. The award consists of a certificate signed by the CMC and a medal set.

3. <u>Eligibility</u>. All civilians are eligible for the SCSA.

4. <u>When Given</u>. An SCSA may be awarded at any time.

5. <u>Criteria</u>. The guidelines for the DCSA will also serve as guidelines for the award of the SCSA. However, for the SCSA, the contributions, which are exceptional in value, would be narrower in scope and/or impact than for the DCSA (e.g., Marine Corps-wide or command wide). The SCSA may be awarded for contributions which serve as a model for other commands.

6. <u>Approval Process</u>. SCSA nominations will be submitted to M&RA (MPC-10) for review and forwarding to the MCIAB for endorsement and forwarding to the CMC.

7. <u>Award Submission Requirements</u>. The format and procedures for submission of recommendations for the SCSA are the same as for the DCSA (see appendix D).

8. <u>Special Requirements</u>. All nominations must include a proposed citation for the SCSA. The language for the citation should not contain superfluous embellishments. The language of the citation should be written in readable conversational language.

9. <u>Records Management</u>. Records documenting Superior Civilian Service Awards submitted to the Commandant of the Marine Corps shall be maintained per reference (d) SSIC 12450.5.

Chapter 5

Meritorious Civilian Service Award

1. General. The Meritorious Civilian Service Award (MCSA) is the third highest honorary award in the Department of the Navy. The contributions that form the basis for this award, while high in value, are more limited in scope and impact than the SCSA.

2. Nature of the Award. The MCSA consists of a certificate and a medal set.

3. Eligibility. All civilians are eligible for the MCSA.

4. When Given. The MCSA may be given at any time.

5. Criteria. The MCSA is conferred for a contribution that applies to a smaller area of operation or a project of lesser importance than one which would warrant consideration for the DCSA or SCSA. The contributions upon which this award is based will be high in value but will be more limited in scope and impact (e.g., command level).

6. Approval Process. Deputy Commandants, Assistant Deputy Commandants, DMCS, and equivalent HQMC staff agency heads may approve the MCSA.

7. Award Submission Requirements. The format and procedures for submission of recommendations are the same as for the MCSA and DCSA (see appendix D). Awards will be submitted directly to the approving authority.

8. Special Requirements. All nominations must include a proposed citation for the MCSA. The language for the citation should not contain superfluous embellishments. The language of the citation should be written in readable conversational language.

9. Records Management. Records documenting Meritorious Civilian Service submitted to the Marine Corps Deputy Commandants and Directors shall be maintained per reference (d), SSIC 12450.1a and 1b as appropriate.

Chapter 6

HQMC Informal Non-Monetary Incentive Awards

1. General Information. Informal incentive awards provide a powerful means to recognize accomplishments of civilians that may otherwise go unrecognized. HQMC encourages supervisors and managers to use informal incentive awards, in addition to other employee award and recognition programs currently available.

2. Eligibility

    a. Informal recognition awards are based on performance or service that is narrower in scope and more limited in application action than that which is generally used as a basis for special act or service awards. It may cover a single task or work assignment that is exceptionally well done or a relatively minor but noteworthy achievement. The award is designed to address those aspects of performance or service which typically go unrecognized but which are worthy of some level of recognition.

    b. All HQMC civilians are eligible to receive informal incentive awards. However, no more than 2 awards may be given to the same individual in any 12 month period. If additional recognition is warranted, other means should be considered.

3. Nature of the Award. An employee receiving an informal incentive award will receive a non-monetary item that will symbolize the employer-employee relationship and will be of some value to the employee to display or use. The following items are available for presentation to civilians as informal incentive awards. All items have the USMC emblem engraved on them:

PEWTER BOWL

JEWELRY BOX

DESK TOP CLOCK

BLACK LEATHER MEMO CASE

CRYSTAL PAPERWEIGHT

4. <u>Nomination/Approval Procedures</u>

    a. Nomination and approval procedures are simplified so that informal recognition awards may be given as soon as possible after the accomplishment that serves as the basis for the award. All supervisors are authorized to nominate civilians for an informal incentive award using the form at appendix E. The justification for an award should be brief.

b. Deputy Commandants, Assistant Deputy Commandants, the Director of Marine Corps Staff, the Director AR Division, and equivalent HQMC staff agency heads (e.g., heads of Office of Legislative Affairs, Safety Division, Public Affairs) are authorized to approve the award and will send the form to the Human Resources and Organizational Management Branch, Employee Management Advisory Services (EMAS) Section. Within one work day of receipt of the NAVMC HQ 961 the organization will be advised to pick up the incentive award for presentation to the civilian.

5. <u>Presentation of the Incentive Award</u>. Organizations are encouraged to present Incentive Awards in an appropriate ceremony. The Incentive Award may be presented as a stand alone award or may be presented in addition to another award or form of recognition (such as a time off award, certificate or letter of commendation or appreciation, etc.).

6. <u>Records Management</u>. Records documenting Informal Non-Monetary Incentive Awards submitted to the Marine Corps Deputy Commandants and Directors and below shall be maintained per reference (d) SSIC 12450.1a and 1b as appropriate.

Chapter 7

Extraordinary Performance Recognition

1. General. An Extraordinary Performance Recognition, which is an increase to base salary, a bonus, or a combination of both, is intended to reward employees when the annual National Security Personnel System (NSPS) performance based payout formula does not adequately compensate the employee for extraordinary performance and results. When an Extraordinary Performance Recognition is made in the form of a salary increase, the extraordinarily high level of performance and results must be expected to continue. Extraordinary Performance Recognitions are made in conjunction with the annual performance payout. Funding for Extraordinary Performance Recognitions is made outside of the pay pool fund.

2. Eligibility. All civilians covered by the NSPS and rated at level 5 are eligible for an Extraordinary Performance Recognition.

3. Determining Award Amounts

    a. In recommending Extraordinary Performance Recognition award amounts, the following factors will be considered:

        (1) Employee's salary in the pay band as compared to other similarly situated employees

        (2) Prior awards and salary increases received during the rating period

        (3) Value of the extraordinary performance and results during the current rating period

    b. In no case may an Extraordinary Performance Recognition in the form of a salary increase cause the employee's pay to exceed the maximum of the pay band or exceed applicable control points, if any, for the position.

4. Approval of Extraordinary Performance Recognition Awards. Recommendations for Extraordinary Performance Recognition Awards will be considered by the Pay Pool Manager during the annual pay pool deliberation process. Use the NAVMC HQ 962 (07-09) (EF) (appendix F) to submit an Extraordinary Performance Recognition

Award nomination. If approved by the Pay Pool Manager, the recommendation will be forwarded to the Performance Review Authority for final approval.

5. Records Management. Records documenting Extraordinary Performance Recognition Awards submitted to the Pay Pool Manager shall be maintained per reference (d) SSIC 12532.9.

Chapter 8

Organization/Team Achievement Recognition

1. <u>General</u>. An Organizational/Team Achievement Recognition is an increase to base salary, a bonus, or a combination of both, and is available to recognize the members of a team, organization, or branch whose performance and contributions have successfully and directly advanced organizational goals. Organizational/Team Achievement Recognition are made in conjunction with the annual NSPS performance payout. Funding for Organizational/Team Achievement Recognitions is made outside of the pay pool fund.

2. <u>Eligibility</u>. Only NSPS employees rated at level 3 and above are eligible for an Organizational/Team Achievement Recognition.

3. <u>Determining Award Amounts</u>

   a. In recommending Organizational/Team Achievement Recognition award amounts, the following factors will be considered:

      (1) Each employee's salary in the pay band as compared to other similarly situated employees.

      (2) Prior awards and salary increases received during the rating period.

   b. Organizational/Team Achievement Recognition award amounts, whether salary, bonus or both, need not be the same for each employee but must, instead, reflect the relative contributions of each member of the team, organization, or branch. In no case may an Organizational/Team Achievement Recognition in the form of a salary increase cause the employee's pay to exceed the maximum of the pay band or exceed applicable control points, if any, for the position.

4. <u>Approval of Organizational/Team Achievement Recognitions</u>. The Pay Pool Manager is authorized to approve Organizational/Team Achievement Recognition recommendations. Use NAVMC HQ 963 (07-09)(EF)(appendix G) to submit an Organizational/Team Achievement Recognition recommendation.

5. <u>Records Management</u>. Records documenting Organization/Team Achievement Recognition submitted to the Pay Pool Manager shall be maintained per reference (d) SSIC 12532.9.

Chapter 9

Armed Forces Civilian Service Medal

1. <u>General</u>. The Armed Forces Civilian Service Medal (AFCSM) is the highest DOD award for a civilian in direct support of military forces engaged in peacekeeping or prolonged humanitarian operations. It is closely aligned with the Armed Forces Medal (AFSM) for military members. The AFCSM may only be awarded for a military operation approved for award of the AFSM for military personnel. The AFCSM may be awarded posthumously and, when so awarded, may be presented to such representative of the deceased as may be deemed appropriate by the Head of the component concerned.

2. <u>Nature of the Award</u>. The award is medal with a lapel pin.

3. <u>Eligibility Requirements</u>

a. Employees must serve in direct support for at least 30 consecutive days or 60 non-consecutive days in the area of eligibility (or for the full period when an operation is of less than 30 days duration) in a military operation awarded the ASFM.

b. The area(s) of eligibility are the same as those designated as approved for the ASFM for military operations, as described below:

(1) The foreign territory on which military troops have actually landed or are present and specially deployed for the operation.

(2) Adjacent water areas in which ships are operating, patrolling, or providing direct support of the operation.

(3) The air space above and adjacent to the area in which operations are being conducted.

4. <u>Submission Requirements</u>. Nomination packages must include the following information:

a. Name of nominee, position, series, grade.

b. Organization.

c. Location of where the employee was working that qualifies him/her for this award.

d. Date of departure to the area of eligibility.

e. Date of return from the area of eligibility.

f. Number of days attached to military unit (or in support of military unit).

5. <u>Limitations on Awarding Medals</u>. The medal may be awarded only to employees of the DOD and only for operations authorized the AFSM for military personnel. No more than one medal may be awarded to any one civilian employee. Participation in subsequent military operations may be acknowledged with a certificate and a 3/16 bronze star. Contribution to, or support of, an AFSM military operation by employees assigned to remotely located activities; e.g., outside the areas of eligibility, is not justification for award of the AFCSM. Such performance or contribution, if merited, may be acknowledged by other appropriate recognition.

6. <u>Submission Requirements and Approval Authority</u>. All nominations for this award must be submitted to M&RA (MPC-10). The CMC is the approving official.

7. <u>Records Management</u>. Records documenting Armed Forces Civilian Service Medal submitted to the Commandant of the Marine Corps shall be maintained per reference (d) SSIC 12450.5.

Chapter 10

Miscellaneous Honorary Awards

1. Letters of Appreciation. Issuing a Letter of Appreciation is a quick way to recognize an employee for a specific short term achievement or excellent customer service. All supervisors are authorized to issue Letters of Appreciation.

2. Certificates of Commendation. Certificates of Commendation are a step above a Letter of Appreciation and usually recognize an exceptional achievement. Branch heads and above are authorized to issue Certificates of Commendation. Certificates are available from HROM.

3. Retirement Awards

   a. All employees retiring with up to 40 years of service are eligible to receive a retirement certificate and letter signed by the CMC.

   b. An employee who retires with 40 or more years of service is eligible to receive a lapel pin, a retirement certificate signed by SECNAV, and a letter signed by the CMC.

   c. Requests for Retirement Awards for those with less than 40 years of service must be submitted to HROM 30 days prior to the date of retirement; requests for Retirement Awards for those with 40 or more years of service must be submitted to HROM 60 days prior to the date of retirement.

4. Records Management. Records documenting awards submitted to the Marine Corps Deputy Commandants and Directors and below shall be maintained per reference (d) SSIC 12450.1a and 1b as appropriate.

5. Department of Defense Global War on Terrorism Medal

   a. The Secretary of Defense Medal for the Global War on Terrorism (GWOT) was created and approved to recognize and honor the contributions and accomplishments of the civilian workforce of the Department of Defense in direct support of the armed forces, whose members are engaged in operations to combat terrorism. The award submission requirements are the same as for the AFCSM. The CMC is the approving official. More information on this award may be found at: http://www.cpms.osd.mil/faslerd/labor_medal.aspx.

b. <u>Records Management</u>. Records documenting Armed Forces
Civilian Service Medal submitted to the Commandant of the Marine
Corps shall be maintained per reference (d) SSIC 12450.5.

Appendix A

Matrix of Approval Authorities for Awards

AWARD	APPROVAL AUTHORITY	OTHER INFORMATION
SPECIAL ACT OR ON THE SPOT		
$25-$750	Division Head or equivalent	
$751-$2,000	Deputy Commandants, the Director of Marine Corps Staff, and equivalent HQMC staff agency heads (e.g., heads of Office of Legislative Affairs, Safety Division, Public Affairs)	
$2,001-$5,000	Director of Marine Corps Staff (via AR Division)	
$5,001-$10,000	CMC	
TIME OFF AWARDS		
1-8 hours	Immediate Supervisor	
9-24 hours	Branch Head	
25-80 hours	Division Head and above	
DISTINGUISHED CIVILIAN SERVICE AWARD	SECNAV	Recommendation is sent to M&RA (MPC-10)
SUPERIOR CIVILIAN SERVICE AWARD	CMC	Recommendation is sent to M&RA (MPC-10)
MERITORIOUS CIVILIAN SERVICE AWARD	Deputy Commandant/ADC, DMCS, equivalent HQMC staff agency heads (e.g., heads of Office of Legislative Affairs, Safety Division, Public Affairs)	
HQMC INFORMAL NON MONETARY INCENTIVE AWARDS	Deputy Commandants, Assistant Deputy Commandants, the Director of Marine Corps Staff, the Director AR Division, and equivalent HQMC staff agency heads (e.g., heads of Office of Legislative Affairs, Safety Division, Public Affairs)	
EXTRAORDINARY PERFORMANCE RECOGNITION	Performance Review Authority (PRA)	Pay Pool Manager must approve prior to forwarding to PRA
ORGANIZATIONAL/TEAM ACHIEVEMENT AWARD	Pay Pool Manager	
ARMED FORCES CIVILIAN SERVICE MEDAL	CMC	Recommendation is sent to M&RA (MPC-10)
LETTERS OF APPRECIATION	Supervisor	
CERTIFICATE OF COMMENDATION	Branch Head and above	
RETIREMENT AWARDS	None	Requests must be submitted 30-60 days in advance of the retirement date
DOD GLOBAL WAR ON TERRORISM MEDAL	CMC	Recommendation is sent to M&RA (MPC-10)

Appendix B

NAVMC HQ 959 (07-09) (EF)
FOUO - Privacy Sensitive when filled in.

Print Form

Special Act and On The Spot Cash Award Nominations

1. **Name of Employee Recommended for Award**		
Last Name	First	MI

2. **Title / Series / Grade**		
Title	Series	Grade

3. **Organization / Code**		4. **Award Amount Recommended**
Organization	Code	Amount

Note: If award is for a group of employees, add a list identifying each employee and the amount of award recommended. Award amounts may vary depending on the relative value of each employee's contribution to the special act or service.

Add List

5. **Justification for the Award**

Provide information on the basis for the award and an explanation of how the award amount was determined.

Add Justification

6. **Record of Nomination and Approvals**

Recommending Official (s)

_____   _____   _____
Title   Signature   Date

_____   _____   _____
Title   Signature   Date

Approving Official

☐ Approved   ☐ Disapproved   Award approved, if other than what was recommended : _____

_____   _____   _____
Title   Signature   Date

Certification that funds are available to pay the award

Funds :   ☐ Are   ☐ Are Not Available   _____   _____
                                              Signature AR, Fiscal   Date

For HROM Use Only

Note : All approvals and the certification of funds are available must be obtained prior to submitting the form to HROM for processing of the award.

Reset Form

Adobe Designer 8.0

Appendix B

NAVMC HQ 959 (07-09) (EF)

Names of Empolyees Recommended for Award	Recommended Time Off Hours

Back

FOR OFFICIAL USE ONLY.

Appendix B

NAVMC HQ 959 (07-09) (EF)

Justification for the award. The justification for the award must contain both the basis for the award and an explanation of how the award amount was determined.

Basis for the nomination. Keep in mind that special act/service awards are not based on general overall performance during a rating period but are based on a specific act or service the employee performed that is worthy of recognition. An example of a special act/service is exceptional work on a special project or while on detail, or performing assigned responsibilities in an exceptional manner under difficult, unusual, and/or complicated circumstances. Be as specific as possible as to what the employee did, describe any obstacles the employee had to overcome in performing the act or service; and address the impact/significance of the employee's contributions.

How the award amount was determined. If you can identify tangible benefits (e.g., the special act or service saved the government xxx dollars), then use the awards table for tangible benefits. If the benefits are intangible, then use the table for intangible benefits, identifying both the extent and value of the employee's contribution. In some cases, there may be both tangible and intangible benefits. If so, describe both in explaining how the recommended award amount was determined. When using the table for intangible benefits, you will see there is a range for the award amount. If you are recommending an award amount at the high end of the range, explain why you are recommending the higher-end award amount.

Enclosure (1)

Appendix C

NAVMC HQ 960 (07-09) (EF)
FOUO - Privacy Sensitive when filled in.

Print Form

Time Off Award Nominations

1. Name of Employee Recommended for Award		
Last Name	First	MI

2. Title / Series / Grade		
Title	Series	Grade

3. Organization / Code		4. Time Off Award Hours Recommended
Organization	Code	Hours

Note: If award is for a group of employees, add a list identifying each employee and the number of time off hours recommended. Time off hours may vary depending on the relative value of each employee's contribution to the special act or service.

Add List

5. Justification for the Award. Provide information on the basis for the award.

6. Record of Nomination and Approvals

Recommending Official (s)

_____   _____   _____
Title   Signature   Date

_____   _____   _____
Title   Signature   Date

Approving Official

[ ] Approved   [ ] Disapproved   Time off hours approved, if other than what was recommended : _____

_____   _____   _____
Title   Signature   Date

For HROM Use Only

Reset Form

FOR OFFICIAL USE ONLY.

Adobe Designer 8.0

Appendix C

NAVMC HQ 960 (07-09) (EF)

Names of Empolyees Recommended for Award	Recommended Time Off Hours

Back

Appendix D

Format for Submitting a Nomination for a Distinguished Civilian
Service Award (DCSA)

1. Nomination packages for the DCSA must include:

    a. A complete description of the employee's service and contributions that form the basis of the award. A specific and detailed report of the employee's accomplishments must include a thorough comparison of how the accomplishments exceeded the employee's job requirements and exceeded the accomplishments of comparable employees with similar job requirements.

    b. An account of the specific benefits, tangible and intangible, which have accrued from the contribution. If the employee's accomplishment result in cost savings, the amount saved must be stated. If intangible benefits have resulted, the specific benefits must be described in detail, with an explanation of the conditions before and after the employee's contributions were implemented.

    c. A description of any award or recognition the employee received as a result of the contributions.

    d. A proposed citation.

    e. The original nomination, signed by the commander, must be submitted.

2. Recommendations must be submitted in the format below:

    a. Resume of one page or less limited to the following information:

        (1) Employee's name, job title, and grade.

        (2) Description of employee's current job responsibilities.

        (3) Summary of nominee's employment history, Federal and non-Federal.

(4) Summary of nominee's educational accomplishments during her/his tenure of Marine Corps employment.

(5) Published papers, articles or books, inventions, participation in professional and civic organizations.

(6) Awards received including date and dollar amount.

b. Narrative justification for the award not to exceed two pages which should include:

(1) Areas of achievement upon which the nomination is based.

(2) Scope and importance of mission, function, service, or task affected compared to normal job expectancy.

(3) Description of ingenuity, innovation, or dedication demonstrating initiatives which exceeded job requirements.

(4) Results achieved, including benefits to the Government, and impact on the organization.

c. Proposed citation to appear on the certificate which must:

(1) State the nominee's name exactly as it should appear on the certificate;

(2) State clearly, accurately, in non-technical unembellished language, the reason for granting the award.

NAVMC HQ 961 (07-09) (EF)
FOUO - Privacy Sensitive when filled in.

| Print Form |

Nomination For An Informal HQMC Incentive Award

1. Nominee Information

Last Name	First	MI

Organization

Justification for the Award

2. Award Item Selected

- ☐ Pewter Bowl
- ☐ Jewelry Box
- ☐ Desk Top Clock
- ☐ Black Leather Memo Case
- ☐ Crystal Paperweight

3. Name of Person HROM Should Contact for Pick Up of Award

Last Name	First

Phone Number	E-mail address

4. Record of Nomination and Approval

Title	Nominating Official	Signature	Date

Title	Approving Official	Signature	Date

For HROM Use Only

Date Approved Nomination Received in HROM	Award Item Issued	Date Item Provided

| Reset Form | FOR OFFICIAL USE ONLY. | Adobe Designer 8.0 |

Appendix F

NAVMC HQ 962 (07-09) (EF)
FOUO - Privacy Sensitive when filled in.

Print Form

Nominations for an Extraordinary Performance Recognition Award

Information About the Employee			
Last Name	First		MI
Title	Organization		

Pay Schedule / Band	Current Salary	Salary Range for the Pay Band	Recommended Rating Prior to Rounding

List all pay increases and awards received by the employee during the period upon which the current rating is based.

Justification for the Award : On a Separate Sheet and Supplementing What is in the Recommended Rating, Describe What Contributions the Employee Made That Are of an Exceedingly High Value to the Organization.

Add Justification

What is being Recommended?

Record of Approvals (and Certification that Level of Performance is Expected to Continue if Salary Increase is Recommended)   Salary Increase of : _____   Bonus of : _____

Rating Official

_____   _____   _____
Name   Signature   Date

Reviewing Official

_____   _____   _____
Name   Signature   Date

To Be Completed by the Pay Pool Manager

Final rating prior to rounding : _____

Amount of performance based increase for current rating period   Salary : _____   Bonus : _____

Recommendation for EPR   ☐ Approved   ☐ Disapproved   Salary increase of : _____   Bonus of : _____

Pay Pool Manager

_____   _____   _____
Name   Signature   Date

Performance Review Authority

☐ Approved   Amount approved, if other than what was recommended : _____   Bonus : _____

☐ Disapproved

_____   _____
Signature, Chairman, PRA   Date

Reset Form

Appendix F

NAVMC HQ 962 (07-09) (EF)

Justification :
Supplementing What is in the Recommended Rating, Describe What Contributions the Employee Made That Are of an Exceedingly High Value to the Organization.

[Back]

FOR OFFICIAL USE ONLY.

Appendix G

NAVMC HQ 963 (07-09) (EF)
FOUO - Privacy Sensitive when filled in.

Print Form

Nomination for an Organizational / Team Achievement Recognition Award

Name of Team, Organization or Branch

On a Separate Sheet, Provide the Following Information About Each Member of the Team Being Recommended for an OAR :

    A. Name

    B. Band / Pay Schedule

    C. All Pay Increases and Awards Received That Were Based in Whole or in Part on the Team Achievements

    D. Specific Salary and / or Bonus Increase Recommended for Each Individual Team Member for the OAR

Add Information

On a Separate Sheet, Provide a Justification for the OAR Recommendation. The Justification Must Include :

How the Team's Performance and Contributions Successfully and Directly Advanced Organizational Goals. Specifically Identify the Organizational Goals Affected by the Team.

If Different Amounts Are Being Recommended for Members of the Team Who are in the Same Pay Schedule / Pay Band, an Explanation of the Reasons for the Differences.

Add Justification

Record of Approvals

Rating Official

| Name | Signature | Date |

Reviewing Official

| Name | Signature | Date |

Action by Pay Pool Manager

☐ Approved   ☐ Disapproved

| Signature | Date |

If Award Amounts Differ From Recommended Amounts, Show Approved Amounts

Reset Form   FOR OFFICIAL USE ONLY.   Adobe Designer 8.0

Appendix G

NAVMC HQ 963 (07-09) (EF)

Member Information :			
A. Name	B. Band / Pay Schedule	C. All Pay Increases and Awards Received That Were Based in Whole or in Part on the Team Achievements	D. Specific Salary and / or Bonus Increase Recommended for Team Member for the OAR

Back

www.ingramcontent.com/pod-product-compliance
Lightning Source LLC
Chambersburg PA
CBHW080610290526

45790CB00007B/2715